Here Comes Mr. Eventoff with the Mail!

written by
ALICE K. FLANAGAN

photographs by
CHRISTINE OSINSKI

Reading Consultant
LINDA CORNWELL
Learning Resource Consultant
Indiana Department of Education

CHILDREN'S PRESS® *A Division of Grolier Publishing*
New York • London • Hong Kong • Sydney • Danbury, Connecticut

Special thanks to Pat Eventoff for allowing us to tell his story.

Also thanks to Timothy Hushion, Postmaster of Ridgefield, Connecticut, and the management staff for their cooperation and support during the making of this book.

Author's Note:
Mr. Eventoff's last name is pronounced E-van-toff.

Library of Congress Cataloging-in-Publication Data
Flanagan, Alice.
   Here comes Mr. Eventoff with the mail! / written by Alice K. Flanagan ; photographs by Christine Osinski ; reading consultant, Linda Cornwell.
      p. cm. — (Our neighborhood series)
   Summary: Follows a letter carrier for a day at his job from the time he arrives at the post office to pick up and sort the mail until the last item is delivered.
   ISBN 0-516-20776-8 (lib.bdg.)   0-516-26405-2 (pbk.)
   1. Postal service—Letter carriers—Juvenile literature.
2. Occupations—Juvenile literature. [1. Postal service—Letter carriers.
2. Occupations.] I. Osinski, Christine, ill. II. Title. III. Series: Our neighborhood (New York, N.Y.)
HE6161.F55 1998
383'.45'0973—dc21   97-32646
                                             CIP
                                             AC

Photographs ©: Christine Osinski

How does a letter that you've written get from the mailbox to your friend?

Let's follow a letter carrier through his day from the beginning to the end.

In the morning, Mr. Eventoff checks in at the post office. Other workers have already picked up the mail from the mailboxes and sorted it by routes.

Mr. Eventoff sorts the mail in his route by name and street number. Sorting can take several hours. If he's not careful, the mail will get mixed up!

Before he leaves to deliver the mail,
Mr. Eventoff checks his truck.
Do the lights work?

8

Do the tires need air? Are there any dents that weren't there yesterday?

He loads the
mail onto
the truck...

…and drives away on his daily route.

Every day, Mr. Eventoff drives the same route through the neighborhood.

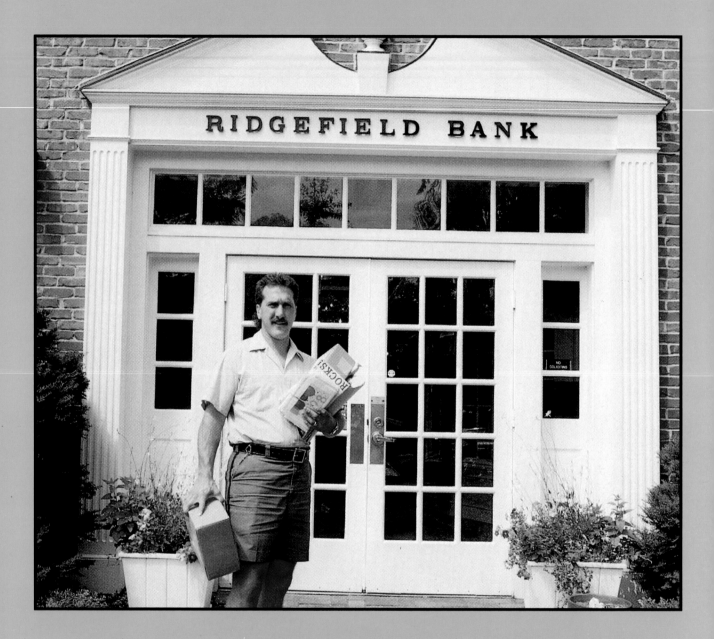

He stops at the bank...

…and at a store. These are just some of the three hundred stops he makes each day.

Delivering mail is hard work.
Mr. Eventoff lifts and carries
heavy loads.

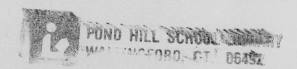

He gets in and out of his truck
many times.

And he's on his feet a lot!

Being friendly is part of Mr. Eventoff's job. He knows every business and family in the neighborhood. He calls each customer by name.

Mr. Eventoff is dependable. He delivers mail even in bad weather or when there are barking dogs.

His customers trust him to keep
their mail safe.

They don't want the mail to get lost
or be put in the wrong place.

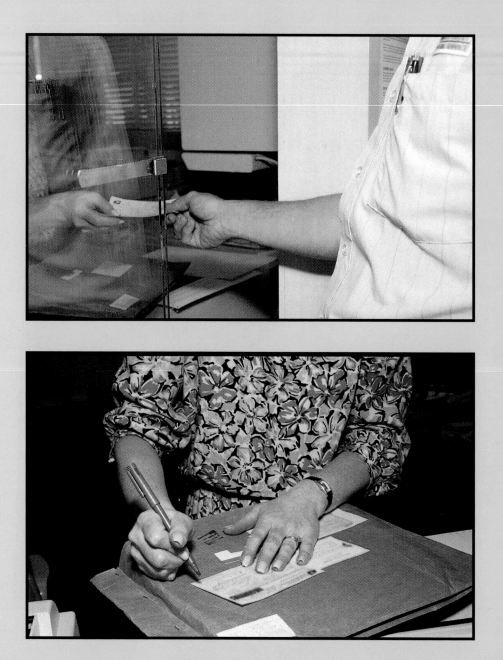

Sometimes, very special mail is sent in a special way. Then, Mr. Eventoff asks customers to sign their name before he gives them the mail.

Mr. Eventoff likes delivering mail. He likes bringing people news and the things they need for their daily lives.

He likes driving his truck. He likes working outside.

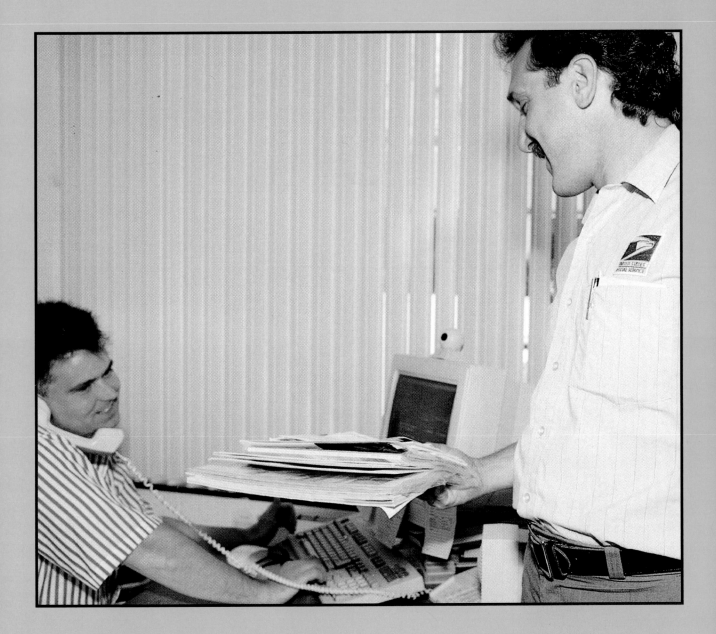

Most of all, Mr. Eventoff likes seeing his customers every day.

At one of the last stops on his route, Mr. Eventoff delivers a surprise.

"Hi, Stephan," Mr. Eventoff says.

"I've brought you a letter.
Could it be from your friend?"

217 Linden Drive
Hollis, Mass. 23844

Stephan Barns
490
Ridg

Meet the Author
and the Photographer

Alice Flanagan and Christine Osinski are sisters. They grew up together telling stories and drawing pictures in a brown brick bungalow in a southwest-side neighborhood of Chicago, Illinois. Today they write stories and take photographs professionally.

Ms. Flanagan resides in Chicago with her husband and works as a freelance writer. Ms. Osinski is a photographer and teaches at The Cooper Union for the Advancement of Science and Art in New York City. She lives with her husband and two sons in Ridgefield, Connecticut.